WONDERS OF THE WEST

by
John Smallwood

SCHOLASTIC INC.

Cover left: Stephen Dunn/Getty Images; center: Garrett Ellwood/NBAE via Getty Images;
right: Andrew D. Bernstein/NBAE via Getty Images

Interior 1: D. Clarke Evans/NBAE via Getty Images; 3: Larry W. Smith/Pool/Getty Images; 4: Ronald Martinez/
Getty Images; 5: Andrew D. Bernstein /NBAE via Getty Images; 6: Garrett W. Ellwood/NBAE via Getty Images;
7: Rocky Widner/NBAE via Getty Images; 8: Andrew D. Bernstein/NBAE via Getty Images; 9: Sam Forencich/
NBAE via Getty Images; 10: Melissa Majchrzak/NBAE via Getty Images; 11: Andrew D. Bernstein/NBAE via
Getty Images; 12: Rocky Widner/NBAE via Getty Images; 13: Nathaniel S. Butler/NBAE via Getty Images; 14:
Danny Bollinger/NBAE via Getty Images; 15: Steven Freeman/NBAE via Getty Images; 16: Rocky Widner/
NBAE via Getty Images; 17: Greg Nelson /Sports Illustrated/Getty Images; 18: Andrew D. Bernstein/NBAE
via Getty Images; 19: Bill Baptist/NBAE via Getty Images; 20: Joe Murphy/NBAE via Getty Images; 21: Brian
Babineau/NBAE via Getty Images; 22: Joe Murphy/NBAE via Getty Images; 23: Greg Nelson/Sports Illustrated/
Getty Images.

Cover Design: Cheung Tai
Interior Design: Rocco Melillo

ISBN 978-0-545-36759-2

12 11 10 9 8 7 6 5 4 3 2 1   13 14 15 16 17 18/0
Printed in the U.S.A.   40

First printing, January 2013

WESTERN CONFERENCE

The San Antonio Spurs posted the best regular season record but lost to the Oklahoma City Thunder in the Western Conference Finals in 2012.

The Thunder beat the 2011 NBA champion Dallas Mavericks and 2010 champion Los Angeles before besting the Spurs to reach their first NBA Finals.

WESTERN CONFERENCE CHAMPIONS

The Oklahoma City Thunder won the 2011–12 Western Conference Championship.

NORTHWEST DIVISION

Led by All-Stars Kevin Durant and Russell Westbrook, the Oklahoma City Thunder won their second straight division championship in 2011–12. The Denver Nuggets and Utah Jazz also qualified for the playoffs.

DENVER NUGGETS

Ty Lawson

Many people thought it was the end for the Denver Nuggets in 2011. No team trades its superstar player and gets better! That, however, is exactly what happened when the Nuggets moved All-Star Carmelo Anthony to the New York Knicks last season.

After Carmelo left, second-year point guard Ty Lawson and 22-year-old forward Danilo Gallinari (acquired from the Knicks) stepped up their games to fill the void that had been left on the Nuggets. Denver won 38 games and made the playoffs in 2011–12.

Because of his size, Ty, who is 5-11, slipped to the 18th pick in 2009 even though he was the most accomplished point guard in the draft and had led the University of North Carolina to the 2009 NCAA Championship. But in three pro seasons, Ty has held his own in the NBA. Last season, the dynamic point guard averaged a career-high 16.4 points and 6.6 assists. In the playoffs, he averaged 19.0 points and 6.0 assists.

Danilo, who was drafted sixth overall in 2008 out of Italy, moved into Carmelo's position as small forward. In just his second game with Denver, he nearly matched his career-high with 30 points. He missed 23 games with an injury but still averaged 14.6 points and shot 32.8 percent on three-pointers.

The Nuggets added center JaVale McGee and hard-working rebounder Kenneth Faried last season to give them one of the more athletic teams in the Western Conference.

NUGGETS 1|0|1

Did you know that in 2010–11 Denver won 50 games for the fourth straight season?

MINNESOTA TIMBERWOLVES

MINNESOTA TIMBERWOLVES

Kevin Love

The Minnesota Timberwolves had placed their future in the hands of a teenage big man before. In 1995, the T-Wolves drafted 19-year-old Kevin Garnett out of Farragut Academy in Chicago, making him the first player in 20 years selected right out of high school. K.G. spent most of his Hall of Fame career in Minneapolis, leading the T-Wolves to their only eight playoff appearances.

Minnesota didn't go back to high school in 2008, but 19-year-old Kevin Love spent just one season at UCLA before entering the 2008 NBA Draft. Kevin was actually drafted fifth overall by the Memphis Grizzlies but was immediately traded to Minnesota.

Like a lot of rookies, Kevin struggled to adjust to the NBA. Though he did not make the Rookie Challenge at All-Star Weekend, Kevin averaged 11.1 points and 9.1 rebounds as a rookie and increased that to 14.0 points and 11.0 rebounds in his second season. In the summer of 2010, Kevin played on the United States team that won the FIBA World Championship. Kevin took his breakout success in 2010–11 to superstar status last season when he averaged a career-high 26.0 points with 13.3 rebounds. A versatile big man, Kevin shot 37.2 percent on three-point shots making him extremely difficult to defend.

He was again named to the NBA All-Star Team and was a member of the 2012 United States team at the Olympics in London.

WOLVES 101

Did you know that Kevin is the first NBA player to average 20 points and 15 rebounds since Moses Malone in 1982–83?

OKLAHOMA CITY THUNDER

After an outstanding first season in 2007–08, Kevin Durant was named 2008 NBA Rookie of the Year and quickly proved himself one of the Oklahoma City Thunder's most valuable players. Kevin is a scoring machine who averaged 30.1 points in 2009–10, becoming the youngest scoring champion in NBA history at age 21. Over five seasons he's averaged 26.3 points while shooting 46.8 percent from the floor.

Although Russell Westbrook was officially the team's last first-round draft pick in 2008, he, too, quickly showed what he could bring to the Thunder. Russell is a true combo guard who averaged 23.6 points and 5.5 assists last season, and he is one of the quickest players in the league who fearlessly attacks the basket.

In the 2011–12 season, Kevin and Russell led the Thunder to the NBA Finals before losing to Miami. In the summer, the duo represented the United States on the 2012 Olympic team. Now they are back looking to bring a title to Oklahoma City.

THUNDER 101

Did you know Oklahoma City was home to the New Orleans Hornets for two seasons after Hurricane Katrina?

Kevin Durant

PORTLAND TRAIL BLAZERS

LaMarcus Aldridge

The Portland Trail Blazers forward/center LaMarcus Aldridge is a perfect example of a player who waited patiently for his chance and then grabbed it. Selected second overall in the 2006 Draft by the Chicago Bulls out of the University of Texas, LaMarcus was traded to the Blazers. He had a solid rookie season until he missed the final 19 games of the regular season due to a medical condition.

LaMarcus came back in 2007–08 as Portland's starting power forward and averaged 17.8 points and 7.6 rebounds. He continued to improve each season and in 2010–11 came in second for the NBA's Most Improved Player.

Last season, LaMarcus made his first All-Star Team. He averaged 21.7 points and 8.0 rebounds while shooting a career best 51.2 percent. But the Blazers missed the playoffs for the first time in three seasons.

During LaMarcus' time in Portland, the Blazers lost promising young center Greg Oden and three-time All-Star Brandon Roy to career-threatening injuries.

This season, Portland is a team undergoing a transition. With two lottery picks they selected Weber State point guard Damian Lillard and Illinois center Meyers Leonard. They added a third first-round pick in Victor Claver, a small forward from Spain who was drafted in 2009.

But with LaMarcus as the leader, the Blazers will again be capable of contending for a playoff spot.

BLAZERS 101

Did you know that until the Portland Timbers joined Major League Soccer in 2011, the Blazers were the only major league franchise in Oregon for 40 years?

UTAH JAZZ

Gordon Hayward believed he would be average height, so while growing up playing basketball in Indiana, his father constantly had him work on the skills that would make him a good point guard.

Just 5-11 when he entered high school, Gordon considered giving up basketball and focusing on playing tennis, a sport in which he was highly ranked in the state. But between his freshman and sophomore years, Gordon had a growth spurt that put him at 6-3, and by his senior year he was 6-8. Even better, he still retained all those skills he had worked on when he thought he was a guard.

Gordon went to Butler University and led the upstart Bulldogs to the 2010 NCAA Championship game where they lost by two points to Duke. Ready to test himself in the NBA, Gordon entered the 2010 Draft and was picked ninth overall by the Jazz.

The 2010–11 season was one of change for Utah. Long-time coach Jerry Sloan retired, and then star point guard Deron Williams was traded to the Nets.

Like a lot of rookies, Gordon struggled while adjusting to the NBA. But last season he doubled his scoring average to 11.8 points and helped Utah return to the playoffs.

Along with powerful center Al Jefferson and versatile wing man Paul Milsaps, Gordon is looking to help the Jazz return to its glory days with John Stockton and Karl Malone rocking Salt Lake City.

Al Jefferson

JAZZ 101

Did you know that the Jazz made the playoffs for 20 straight seasons between 1984 and 2004?

PACIFIC DIVISION

The Los Angeles Lakers won the division in 2011–12 but only by a game over their city-rivals, the Clippers, who also made the playoffs.

GOLDEN STATE WARRIORS

Sometimes a team has to take a chance to move things forward. That's what the Golden State Warriors did when they traded high-scoring guard Monta Ellis to the Milwaukee Bucks for injured center Andrew Bogut. When healthy, Andrew has been a solid NBA big man, averaging 12.7 points, 9.3 rebounds, and 1.6 blocks for his career. But he has missed significant time due to injury in each of the past four seasons.

Still, if Andrew comes through, the Warriors could be on to something. Andrew was the first non-American player to win the Naismith Award as college basketball's top player, and was picked first overall by Milwaukee in 2005.

Golden State already has a high-scoring front court player in forward David Lee, who averaged 20.1 points and 9.6 rebounds last season. And with guard Stephen Curry, they have another player capable of putting up 20 points a game. The development of 2011 first pick Klay Thompson made it possible to trade Monta Ellis, and the 6-7 swingman should complement Stephen in the backcourt. The Warriors also drafted 6-8 power forward Harrison Barnes seventh overall out of the University of North Carolina.

It could be tough for the Warriors to move up in the powerful Western Conference. But they've made changes that have them looking toward a title.

Andrew Bogut

WARRIORS 101

Did you know that in the 2007 Playoffs, the Warriors beat the Dallas Mavericks to become the first number-eight seed to beat a number-one seed in a seven-game series?

12

LOS ANGELES CLIPPERS

Blake Griffin

His arrival was a year later than everyone expected, but when Blake Griffin finally hit the NBA, it was like a supernova. After missing his true rookie season because of a knee injury, Blake showed why the Los Angeles Clippers drafted him first overall in 2009: He was incredible. At 6-10, the former Oklahoma Sooner played the game with power and force, averaging 22.5 points, which was the highest rookie scoring average since Allen Iverson in 1996–97.

But that wasn't all. Blake averaged 12.1 rebounds, which was the most for a rookie since Shaquille O'Neal in 1992–93. Blake also became the first rookie since Elton Brand in 1999–2000 to average at least 20 points and 10 rebounds. And he was the first rookie to make the All-Star game since Yao Ming in 2003.

But that still wasn't all. Blake became the first unanimous pick for Rookie of the Year since David Robinson in 1990. And in a personal best, Blake won the Slam Dunk contest at All-Star Weekend after he jumped over a car to dunk.

Last season, he was teamed with All-Star point guard Chris Paul and helped lead the Clippers to the playoffs for just the second time in 15 seasons. By adding veterans Jamal Crawford, Lamar Odom, and Grant Hill, the Clippers might make a deep run into the playoffs.

CLIPPERS 101

Did you know that the Clippers franchise has had five rookies of the year, but Blake is the first since the move to Los Angeles from San Diego in 1984?

LOS ANGELES LAKERS

Kobe Bryant has been underestimated before. When the Los Angeles Lakers won only 34 games and missed the playoffs in 2005, it appeared that the dynasty had ended. But Kobe thought otherwise.

He stayed in Los Angeles to build the Lakers back to greatness, and when the team acquired forward Pau Gasol from the Memphis Grizzlies in 2008, "Showtime" was back in Los Angeles. Kobe and Pau clicked immediately, and in 2009 the Lakers beat the Orlando Magic for the NBA Championship and again in 2010 against the Celtics. Kobe joined NBA franchise legends George Mikan, Kareem Abdul-Jabbar, and Magic Johnson by winning five championships for the Lakers.

But Kobe wants that sixth championship, and after the Lakers traded with the Phoenix Suns for two-time MVP Steve Nash, he could be in a position to get it. Kobe came to the Lakers in 1996 as an 18-year-old just out of high school. He is the franchise's all-time leading scorer with 27,868 points, the sixth-highest amount in NBA history. Pau, who is from Spain, made the Finals his first season with the Lakers. He averaged more than 18 points and 10 rebounds during the 2009 and 2010 Playoffs.

The Lakers didn't win the championship last season. But with Kobe, Pau, and now Steve, they are a force to be reckoned with.

Kobe Bryant

LAKERS 101

Did you know that the Lakers won five NBA titles in Minneapolis before they moved to Los Angeles in 1960?

PHOENIX SUNS

Kendall
Marshall

How do you replace a legendary player who was the face of your franchise?

You don't—at least not right away. But you start with a player who has the confidence to do so. The Suns didn't draft University of North Carolina point guard Kendall Marshall 13th overall with the belief that he was going to be Steve Nash—the two-time NBA MVP who was traded to the Los Angeles Lakers. That would not be fair. But in Kendall, the Suns saw a player with the potential to develop into someone who could guide them into the next phase of their history.

In his two seasons at North Carolina, Kendall, 6-3, showed that he was a classic point guard with teamsmanship being first in his mind. As a sophomore, Kendall averaged 9.8 assists and won the Bob Cousy Award as the best point guard in college basketball.

Once in Phoenix, Kendall will have plenty of opportunities to complement big men like center Marcin Gortat, who averaged 15.4 points and 10.0 rebounds last season, and second-year forward Markieff Morris, a 6-10 bruiser who helped lead Kansas to the 2011 NCAA championship game.

The Suns have also added former Minnesota Timberwolves forward Michael Beasley who is looking for a fresh start. The transition from the Steve Nash era will be slow for the Suns, but in Kendall, they have a young player who is ready to lead the way.

SUNS 101

Did you know that Kendall is the third Tar Heel to win the Bob Cousy Award, joining current NBA players Raymond Felton (2005) and Ty Lawson (2009)?

SACRAMENTO KINGS

Tyreke Evans

Tyreke Evans stood in lofty company after his rookie season with the Sacramento Kings. Drafted fourth overall in 2009, Tyreke joined Oscar Roberston, Michael Jordan, and LeBron James as the only rookies to average at least 20 points, 5.0 rebounds, and 5.0 assists. The combination guard out of the University of Memphis was the MVP of the 2010 Rookie Challenge at All-Star weekend and 2010 NBA Rookie of the Year.

But in 2010–11, Tyreke had a setback: an injury to his left foot that made him miss games. He bounced back last season averaging 16.5 points and 4.6 rebounds. The Kings are rebuilding the franchise, with Tyreke being a key member of a young core. In 2010, the Kings drafted University of Kentucky freshman center DeMarcus Cousins as the fifth overall pick. Like Tyreke, DeMarcus worked his way into the starting lineup. He averaged 14.1 points and 8.6 rebounds and was named First Team All-Rookie. Last season, DeMarcus showed he was one of the best centers in the league by averaging 18.1 points and 11.0 rebounds.

Back in the early 2000s, the Kings, led by an inside/outside combination of Chris Webber and Mike Bibby, were one of the top teams in the league. They won 50 games for five straight seasons. As Sacramento moves forward, Tyreke and DeMarcus could be the new combination that brings back that success.

KINGS 101

Did you know that the franchise joined the NBA as the Rochester (New York) Royals in 1948 and is one of the oldest basketball clubs in existence?

SOUTHWEST DIVISION

The San Antonio Spurs got off to a terrific start, posting a Western Conference best of 50 victories to win the division in 2011–12.

The Memphis Grizzlies and Dallas Mavericks also made the playoffs.

DALLAS MAVERICKS

Dirk Nowitzki

Before 1996, no international player without at least some NCAA experience had ever been selected in the Top 10 of the NBA Draft. Dirk Nowitzki was just 18 years old and from Germany, a nation that had produced thousands of great soccer players but only one great NBA player—three-time All-Star Detlef Schrempf. Taking a chance on Dirk was a huge risk, but the Dallas Mavericks knew something nobody else did.

Dirk, who was selected ninth overall by the Milwaukee Bucks and then immediately traded to Dallas in a prearranged deal, has not only become the greatest European player in NBA history. He's simply one of the greatest players in the NBA.

After leading the Mavericks to their first NBA Championship in 2011, Dirk's legacy was secured. But it did not happen right away. Dirk struggled with a new style of play in the NBA (European basketball does not allow as much contact) and he played in just 47 games as a rookie. But the next season he started 81 of 82 games and increased his scoring average to 17.5 points. After two years of adjustment, Dirk became the Mavericks' star player in 2000–01. He has averaged at least 21 points for 12 straight seasons.

A 10-time NBA All-Star, Dirk has been named All-NBA First Team four times and All-NBA Second Team five times. He was the MVP of the 2011 NBA Finals and 23rd on the all-time scoring list with 22,792 points.

MAVERICKS 101

Did you know Dirk was the first European player to be named NBA MVP in 2007?

HOUSTON ROCKETS

Jeremy Lin

All of last season, as the Houston Rockets watched "LinSanity" sweep through New York, they knew they had made a mistake. Just before the start of the 2011–12 season, the Rockets signed point guard Jeremy Lin off of waivers and had him at training camp. Jeremy played seven minutes in the preseason but was cut the day before Christmas. Three days later, Lin, who played at Harvard University but was not drafted, was signed by the New York Knicks as a backup. He played a few minutes of a preseason game but was then sent to the NBA Development League. In January, the Knicks were thinking about cutting Lin, but he was put in the fourth quarter of a game and showed he could play.

On February 4, 2012, in a game against the Nets, Jeremy had 25 points and 7 rebounds. The madness had begun and became known as "Linsanity." Jeremy played wonderfully for the Knicks, scoring big points and making game-winning shots. In February, he was named NBA Eastern Conference Player of the Week after averaging 27.3 points and 8.0 assists in four Knicks victories.

With Jeremy playing well, the Knicks turned their season around and made the playoffs. Unfortunately, a knee injury ended Jeremy's season early. But in the 29 games he played, he averaged 14.6 points and 6.2 assists. He became popular around the world.

The Rockets signed Jeremy as a free agent last summer in hopes that he will bring the same kind of excitement to Houston.

ROCKETS 101

Did you know the Rockets won back-to-back NBA championships in the '90s (1994, 1995)?

MEMPHIS GRIZZLIES

Sometimes a player just has to find the right home to become successful. Zach Randolph had done well playing with the Portland Trail Blazers, the New York Knicks, and the Los Angeles Clippers. Still, things had never seemed to be quite right.

But in 2009, success came for Zach with the most unlikely franchise. The Memphis Grizzlies were coming off three straight seasons of fewer than 25 wins. Though Memphis had a young emerging star in swingman Rudy Gay, they needed an inside force to take things to the next level.

Zach was that player. In his first season in Memphis, Zach averaged 20.8 points and 11.7 rebounds. He also made his first All-Star team. In the same season, Rudy Gay averaged 19.6 points and 5.9 rebounds and shot a career-high 46.6 percent. Most importantly, the Grizzlies won 40 games and took a huge step forward.

In 2010–11, with Zach (averaging 20.1 points and 12.2 rebounds per game) and Rudy (averaging 19.8 points per game) leading the way, Memphis won its first playoff series.

Troubled by injuries in the 2011–12 season, Zach only played 28 regular season games. He averaged 11.6 points and 8.0 rebounds, but in the playoffs, those numbers increased to 13.7 points and 9.9 rebounds. With Zach at full strength, Memphis is looking to move up the order in the Western Conference.

GRIZZLIES 101

Did you know the Grizzlies were originally located in Vancouver, British Columbia?

Zach Randolph

NEW ORLEANS HORNETS

Anthony Davis

Going into the 2011–12 season, the New Orleans Hornets did not feel sorry for themselves. Though they were devastated by the trade that sent All-Star point guard Chris Paul to the Los Angeles Clippers, the Hornets fought through the season. And as luck would have it, hope was on the way.

In April 2012, University of Kentucky freshman center Anthony Davis came to New Orleans and showed he was the best player in college basketball by leading the Wildcats to the NCAA Championship. A few months later, Davis was celebrating in New Orleans again as the Hornets selected him with the No. 1 overall pick in the 2012 Draft. After just one season at Kentucky, Davis was labeled a franchise-changer.

Anthony was the Southeastern Conference Player of the Year, the Most Outstanding Player of the NCAA Final Four, and the consensus National Player of the Year. He has been described as having the potential to play defense as well as Hall of Fame center Bill Russell. He also set the NCAA record for blocked shots by a freshman with 186 and had six blocks in the NCAA Championship game.

But Anthony is just the biggest piece of the puzzle. The new-look Hornets resigned high-scoring guard Eric Gordon, who they received in the trade for Paul, and then drafted Duke University point guard Austin Rivers tenth overall. Only time will tell if all the pieces will fit together, leading to a title.

HORNETS 101

Did you know that New Orleans' first NBA team was the Jazz, which played there from 1974 to 1979 before moving to Utah?

SAN ANTONIO SPURS

Nobody ever calls them the "Big Three," but Tim Duncan, Manu Ginobili, and Tony Parker have won more NBA titles than any other trio in the league.

Tim has been the anchor of the San Antonio Spurs since he was selected first overall in the 1997 Draft. Now in his 15th season, Tim, who has averaged 20.3 points, 11.3 rebounds, and 2.2 blocks in his career, led the Spurs to the championship in 1999, 2003, 2005, and 2007. He is arguably the greatest power forward ever. A 13-time All-Star, the native of the Virgin Islands is the only player to be selected All-NBA and All-Defensive team in each of his first 13 seasons.

Hailing from Argentina, Manu was the 57th pick in the 1999 Draft but did not come to the Spurs until 2002. Despite being a sixth man, Manu has career averages of 15.2 points, 4.0 rebounds, and 3.9 assists. He is a two-time All-Star and was the 2008 Sixth Man of the Year. In 2004, Manu led Argentina to the Olympic gold medal.

People didn't know a lot about Tony when San Antonio drafted the 19-year-old point guard from France as the 28th pick in the 2001 Draft. He immediately became the starting point guard, a role he has kept for a decade, and is a three-time All-Star with career averages of 16.8 points and 5.9 assists.

Manu Ginobili

SPURS 101

Did you know San Antonio is the only former ABA team to win the NBA title?

2011-2012 CELEBRATION

NBA WESTERN CONFERENCE CHAMPIONS

Oklahoma City Thunder

NBA WESTERN CONFERENCE

2011-2012 WESTERN CONFERENCE STANDINGS

Spurs	50–16	
Thunder	47–19	
Lakers	41–25	
Grizzlies	41–25	
Clippers	40–26	
Nuggets	38–28	
Mavericks	36–30	
Jazz	36–30	

Rockets	34–32
Suns	33–33
Trailblazers	28–38
T-Wolves	26–40
Warriors	23–43
Kings	22–44
Hornets	21–45

2011-2012
EASTERN CONFERENCE STANDINGS

Bulls	50–16
Heat	46–20
Pacers	42–24
Celtics	39–27
Hawks	40–26
Magic	37–29
Knicks	36–30
Sixers	35–31
Bucks	31–35
Pistons	25–41
Raptors	23–43
Nets	22–44
Cavaliers	21–45
Wizards	20–46
Bobcats	7–59

BEASTS OF THE EAST

by
John Smallwood

HEAT
6

SCHOLASTIC INC.

Cover Design: Cheung Tai
Interior Design: Rocco Melillo

ISBN 978-0-545-36759-2

12 11 10 9 8 7 6 5 4 3 2 1   13 14 15 16 17 18/0
Printed in the U.S.A.   40
First printing, January 2013

EASTERN CONFERENCE

The battle for the 2011–12 NBA Eastern Conference Championship was between the Boston Celtics and the Miami Heat.

The Celtics fought hard, pushing the series to a full seven games. But it was the Heat that won the Eastern Conference Playoffs and went on to win the NBA Championship.

NBA CHAMPIONS

The Miami Heat beat the Oklahoma City Thunder to win the 2011–12 NBA Championship.

ATLANTIC DIVISION

The Boston Celtics, with its Fantastic Four of Ray Allen, Kevin Garnett, Paul Pierce, and Rajon Rondo, won the 2011–12 Atlantic Division for the fourth straight season. The New York Knicks and Philadelphia 76ers joined the Celtics in the playoffs.

BOSTON CELTICS

It's always hard to be in the shadow of a superstar. So imagine how difficult it was for Boston Celtics point guard Rajon Rondo to play in a starting lineup that included future Hall of Fame players Ray Allen, Kevin Garnett, and Paul Pierce.

When Boston brought Kevin, Paul, and Ray together in 2007, Rajon, who was in his second season, was viewed as a question mark who might keep the "Big Three" from a title.

Rajon was just the opposite. He averaged 10.6 points, 5.1 assists, and 4.2 rebounds as the Celtics posted the best record in the NBA in 2007–08. During the 2008 NBA Playoffs, Rajon averaged 10.2 points and 6.6 assists as Boston won its 17th championship.

Rajon has continued to show he is on par with the Big Three. He made his first All-Star team in 2010 and again in 2011 and 2012. In the 2011–12 season, Rajon averaged 11.9 points and 11.7 assists.

The Celtics have been a power team over the past three seasons, winning one title and also reaching the 2010 NBA Finals. Living up to the expectations of his fellow players, Rajon promises to continue the Celtics' legacy of greatness.

Rajon Rondo

CELTICS 101

Did you know that the Celtics won eight straight titles in the 1960s? It was the longest championship streak enjoyed by any North American professional team.

BROOKLYN NETS

BROOKLYN

Deron Williams

The Nets knew in order to dramatically improve they needed to do something drastic. The team wanted an NBA superstar, but there would be a cost. They gave up rookie forward Derrick Favors, veteran point guard Devin Harris, and two future first-round draft picks to the Utah Jazz in order to get Deron Williams. But considering that Deron is one of the top point guards in the NBA, the price was worth it.

Traded to the Nets on February 21, 2011 (when the team was still the New Jersey Nets), Deron had an immediate impact. The Nets became one of the highest scoring teams in the league. In 2012, Deron averaged 21.0 points and 8.7 assists.

Picked third overall in the 2005 Draft out of the University of Illinois to replace the legendary John Stockton, Deron became the Utah Jazz's best player during his five and a half seasons in Salt Lake City. He is a two-time All-Star and a member of the 2008 and 2012 United States Olympic teams.

Although he was a free agent, Deron stayed with the Nets as they transitioned from being the New Jersey Nets to the Brooklyn Nets in 2012. This way he would be the team's main attraction as they began their new history in Brooklyn. With the help of All-Star guard Joe Johnson and talented young center Brook Lopez, Deron is the perfect point guard to make the Nets a team to watch in the 2012–13 season.

NETS 101

Did you know that the Nets have moved to Brooklyn, New York for the 2012–13 season?

New York is a hard city to ignore and a hard place not to be a champion. Knicks fans have waited since 1973 for another NBA title, and both Amar'e Stoudemire and Carmelo Anthony came to New York to make that happen.

Amar'e left the Phoenix Suns in 2010 and immediately became the Knicks' star player, leading them to a 28–26 record at the All-Star break.

Just after the All-Star break, the Knicks acquired Carmelo from the Denver Nuggets in a trade, and New York had its superstar lineup. After a period of adjustment, Amar'e and Carmelo showed the Big Apple what they were capable of by taking the Knicks to the playoffs for the first time since 2004. In 2012, Carmelo averaged 22.6 points and 6.3 rebounds. In the playoffs against the Miami Heat he averaged 27.8 points and 8.2 rebounds. Amar'e missed 18 games due to a back injury but still averaged 17.5 points and 7.8 rebounds.

Last season, the Knicks added center Tyson Chandler to the mix, and this season they brought in veteran point guard Jason Kidd. With these two top players leading the way, the Knicks might finally bring another NBA title to New York.

KNICKS 101

 that the New York Knicks and the Boston Celtics are the only original NBA teams still based in their founding cities?

Amar'e Stoudemire

PHILADELPHIA 76ERS

PHILADELPHIA

Jrue Holiday

It's been a while, but the future seems to have finally arrived for the Philadelphia 76ers. In fourth-year point guard Jrue Holiday, third-year swingman Evan Turner, and center Andrew Bynum, Philadelphia has a group of young stars around which a champion team can be built.

Jrue's rookie season in 2009–10 was a learning experience. At 19, he was the youngest player in the league and only had one season of experience at UCLA. Starting 51 games and averaging 8.0 points and 3.8 assists, Jrue was a tireless competitor. In 2010, he took over as the Sixers' starting point guard and became one of the most improved players in the league. He started 147 straight games, and in the 2012 Playoffs, Jrue averaged 15.8 points and 4.7 rebounds helping the Sixers win a series for the first time since 2003.

The Sixers are looking for Evan to follow a similar path. Selected second overall in the 2010 Draft out of Ohio State, Evan took over as a starter in the backcourt with Jrue late in the season. The pair clicked, and Evan averaged 10.3 points and 6.7 rebounds in 13 playoff games.

Then, in June 2012, the 76ers gained star center Andrew Bynum in a trade from the Lakers. With Jrue, Evan, and Andrew (who helped lead the Lakers to two championships in 2009 and 2010), the Sixers' future is brighter than ever.

SIXERS 101

Did you know that seven 76ers—Charles Barkley, Wilt Chamberlain, Billy Cunningham, Julius Erving, Hal Greer, Moses Malone, and Dolph Schayes—were each voted one of the 50 Greatest in NBA history?

Andrea Bargnani

A team can't lose a talented player without being affected. The Toronto Raptors, having lost Chris Bosh in 2010 to the Miami Heat, were no different. Still, as the Raptors struggled through a period of transition, two young stars—Andrea Bargnani and DeMar DeRozan—emerged with breakout seasons.

In 2006, Andrea, who is from Italy, became the first European player to be selected No. 1 overall in the NBA Draft. Called "Il Mago" (The Magician), the seven-foot power forward has steadily improved over each of his five seasons. In 2008, Andrea changed his game by driving to the basket instead of settling for jump shots. Although he was out with an injury for half of last season, Andrea averaged 19.5 points and 5.5 rebounds in 31 games.

Originally hailing from Compton, California, DeMar quickly became a fan favorite in Toronto. Drafted ninth overall in 2009 out of the University of Southern California, the high-flying shooting guard averaged just 8.6 points as a rookie. Now DeMar has started every game in the past two seasons for the Raptors and averaged nearly 17 points.

The Raptors are a young and growing team, but they have a strong foundation in Andrea and DeMar, who may soon become All-Stars.

RAPTORS 101

Did you know that the Toronto Raptors were established in **1995**, along with the Vancouver Grizzlies, as part of the NBA expansion into Canada?

CENTRAL DIVISION

Led by 2010–11 NBA Most Valuable Player Derrick Rose, the Chicago Bulls won their second consecutive division title in 2012.

The Bulls again topped the Eastern Conference with 50 wins, but an injury to Derrick contributed to their first-round loss to Philadelphia in the playoffs. The Indiana Pacers had the third-best record in the East and moved to the second round of the playoffs.

CHICAGO BULLS

Sometimes the future seems set in stone. Growing up as a basketball player on the South Side of Chicago in the 1990s, Derrick Rose didn't have to look far for inspiration. When Derrick was a toddler, Michael Jordan and the Bulls dynasty captured their first "Three-Peat." Before Derrick was ten, the Bulls had won three more NBA titles. Then Michael Jordan retired and everything stopped.

In the years that followed, the Bulls missed the playoffs for six straight seasons. Every kid in Chicago dreamed of being the basketball player to bring the team back to its greatness.

Derrick became the one to do it. After his freshman season at the University of Memphis, Derrick was selected first overall by the Bulls in the 2008 Draft. He was named Rookie of the Year, and the Bulls made the playoffs for just the third time in eleven seasons. In the 2009–10 season, Derrick made his first All-Star Team, and Chicago again made the playoffs.

In 2010–11, Derrick became the youngest player in NBA history to be named Most Valuable Player at only 22 years old. He and Michael Jordan were the only Bulls to ever win MVP.

Injuries limited Derrick to just 39 games in 2011–12 and one playoff game, but he looks to come back this season in MVP-form. With Derrick, Chicago has made four consecutive playoffs for the first time since Michael Jordan retired.

BULLS 101

Did you know Derrick was born in 1988, the same year Michael Jordan won his first MVP?

Derrick Rose

CLEVELAND CAVALIERS

Kyrie Irving

At the end of the 2010–11 season, the Cleveland Cavaliers were looking to move forward. And that's exactly what they did in the 2011 NBA Draft. With the first overall selection, the Cavaliers picked Duke University freshman point guard Kyrie Irving. Then, with the fourth overall pick, Cleveland drafted University of Texas freshman forward Tristan Thompson. In one night, the Cavaliers, who won just 19 games in 2010–11, made moves to ensure that Cleveland has a NBA Championship in its future.

Kyrie played just 11 games at Duke until he suffered a foot injury. But his performance in those games and his reputation coming into college as a prep All-American caught Cleveland's eye. He averaged 20.5 points and 4.3 assists while shooting 52.9% from the floor, 46.2% on three-pointers, and 90.1% on free throws. Kyrie has drawn comparisons to Los Angeles Clippers All-Star Chris Paul.

Kyrie did not disappoint his first season in Cleveland. He averaged 18.5 points and 5.4 assists to win Rookie of the Year honors.

Tristan, at 6-9 and 235 pounds, is a "corner man"—a player who can play both power and small forward. He averaged 8.2 points and 6.5 rebounds as a rookie.

CAVS 101

Did you know that Kyrie has dual citizenship in the United States and Australia, and that Tristan is a citizen of Canada?

13

DETROIT PISTONS

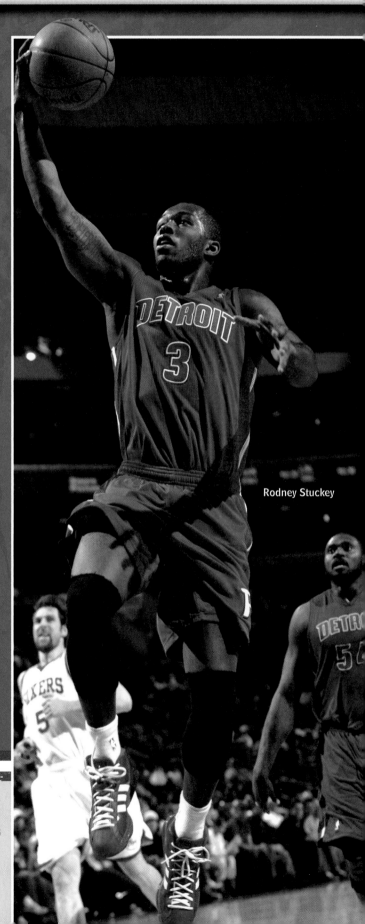

Detroit Pistons general manager Joe Dumars may have seen a little bit of himself in Rodney Stuckey. Like Joe, who played for McNeese State University before joining Detroit for 14 seasons, Rodney entered the NBA Draft with a reputation as a big-time scoring guard from a small college. When Joe had first played, a lot of people questioned his being a first-round pick because of the school he came from. But Joe proved the skeptics wrong and had a strong NBA career. He saw the same promise in Rodney.

As a sophomore at Eastern Washington University, Rodney was seventh in the NCAA with 24.6 points per game, while also averaging 5.5 assists and 2.4 steals. He entered the 2007 Draft, and the Pistons selected him 15th overall. They viewed him as a combination point guard who could score and run an offense.

Rodney hit the NBA running and was elected to the All-Rookie Second Team in 2008. Detroit made the playoffs in Rodney's first two seasons. Last season, Rodney averaged 14.8 points and teamed with center Greg Monroe to give the Pistons a strong outside/inside combination. With Rodney as one of their key players, the Pistons are aiming to return to the playoffs.

Rodney Stuckey

PISTONS 101

Did you know that Rodney joined Joe Dumars and Tayshaun Prince as one of the only rookies to start a playoff game for Detroit?

Danny Granger

When Indiana Pacers President of Basketball Operations Larry Bird, one of the greatest players in NBA history, makes you his first-round pick, there is pressure to succeed.

Both Danny Granger and Tyler Hansbrough have been up to the task. Danny, who was drafted out of the University of New Mexico in 2005, became the Pacers' starting small forward in 2007. He averaged 19.6 points his first season as a starter and then averaged at least 20 points for the next three consecutive seasons. Danny was a member of the 2010 USA Men's National Team that won the gold medal at the 2010 FIBA World Championship.

Tyler stayed at the University of North Carolina for his senior year to help win the 2009 NCAA Championship. Selected 13th overall in the 2009 Draft, his rookie season was limited to 29 games because of a series of inner ear infections. The next season, though, the aggressive forward displayed the tenacity that made him such a fierce competitor in college, and he averaged 11.0 points and 5.2 rebounds.

The Pacers were the surprise team of the 2011–12 Eastern Conference by finishing with the third best record. Indiana beat Orlando in the first round before falling to Miami. With young stars like Danny, Tyler, and center Roy Hibbert, Indiana has the foundation of an elite team.

PACERS 101

Did you know that Danny has the highest single-season scoring average (25.8 points in 2008–09) in Pacers history?

MILWAUKEE BUCKS

Milwaukee Bucks guard Brandon Jennings needed a running mate in the backcourt. Monta Ellis needed a new scene. So when the Bucks traded center Andrew Bogut to the Golden State Warriors as part of an exchange for Monta, both Brandon and Monta saw their chance to become one of the most dynamic backcourt duos in the NBA. Together, Brandon and Monta averaged nearly 40 points and 12 rebounds last season.

In 2008, Brandon, who is from Compton, California, was the top high-school player in the United States. He quickly earned a scholarship to the University of Arizona. But Brandon wanted to be a NBA player. When the NBA's age restriction prevented him from entering the draft, he signed with Lottomatica Roma of the Italian A League. After one season in Italy, Brandon was drafted 10th overall by the Bucks.

Three years earlier, Monta was drafted out of Lanier High School in Jackson, Mississippi, in the second round in 2005. He did not take long to establish himself as one of the top scorers in the NBA. In 2007, he increased his scoring average from 6.8 points as a rookie to 16.5 points and was named NBA Most Improved Player. Earning a reputation as a fearless shooter, Monta poured in points over the next five years. Last season, he averaged 20.4 points.

With Brandon and Monta, Milwaukee is hoping to have the edge they need to return to the playoffs.

BUCKS 101

Did you know that no expansion franchise in American major-league sports has won a title faster than the Bucks? They won the 1971 NBA Championship in their third season.

Brandon Jennings

SOUTHEAST DIVISION

The Miami Heat and its "Big Three" of LeBron James, Dwyane Wade, and Chris Bosh beat the Oklahoma City Thunder to win the NBA Championship. The Orlando Magic and Atlanta Hawks also made the playoffs.

ATLANTA HAWKS

The Atlanta Hawks have had several great players since the franchise relocated from St. Louis in 1968, but they have rarely had them at the same time. Now things are different. In young forwards Josh Smith and Al Horford, the Hawks hope to add another NBA Championship to their legacy.

Al is a 6-10 center/forward who led the University of Florida to the 2006 and 2007 NCAA titles before being selected No. 3 overall in the 2007 NBA Draft. A two-time All-Star, Al played only 11 games last season after tearing a muscle in his chest. But he averaged 15.3 points and 8.3 rebounds as Atlanta challenged Boston in the playoffs.

Josh stepped up his game to All-Star level in 2011–12 by averaging a career-high 18.8 points and 9.6 rebounds. Drafted 17th overall out of Oak Hill Academy by his hometown Hawks, Josh has gradually made the transition from high-school phenomena to NBA superstar. A dynamic defender, he became the youngest player in NBA history to reach 1,000 blocked shots at age 24.

With Josh and Al leading the way, the Hawks have made the playoffs five consecutive times. Atlanta may not have a Big Three like the Boston Celtics and the Miami Heat. But with two of the top players in the NBA, the team has the star power to move forward and make a play for the NBA Finals.

Al Horford

HAWKS 101

Did you know that the Hawks started as the Tri-Cities Blackhawks and were one of the NBA's 17 original teams before moving to Milwaukee, then to St. Louis, and then to Atlanta?

CHARLOTTE BOBCATS

Michael
Kidd-Gilchrist

Some teams just need a player who knows how to win. That's what the Charlotte Bobcats were thinking when they drafted Michael Kidd-Gilchrist with the second overall pick in the 2012 NBA Draft.

Having played just one season at the University of Kentucky, Michael, a 6-7 swingman, helped lead the Wildcats to the NCAA Championship. Head coach John Calipari called Michael the hardest working player on a team that featured four 2012 first-round draft picks.

Michael started 39 of 40 games at Kentucky and averaged 11.9 points and 7.4 rebounds. He was named to the Final Four All-Tournament Team.

In Charlotte, Michael joins young players like Kemba Walker, Bismack Biyombo, and Gerald Henderson who are looking for a positive team identity. Yet Charlotte is coming off a terrible season when they set a record for the worst winning percentage in history and lost their final 23 games.

But in the last two drafts, the Bobcats selected Michael and Kemba primarily because they are players who have helped teams win NCAA Championships in the past.

The Charlotte Bobcats are counting on winning being contagious.

BOBCATS 101

Did you know the Bobcats came to Charlotte as an expansion team in 2004, two seasons after the Hornets relocated to New Orleans?

MIAMI HEAT

When LeBron James and Chris Bosh joined Dwyane Wade on the Miami Heat, their only goal was to win the NBA Championship. Last season, they made that happen. Rebounding from the disappointment of losing the 2011 NBA Finals to the Dallas Mavericks, the Heat, led by LeBron, Chris, and Dwayne, defeated the Oklahoma City Thunder in 2012 in five games.

During seven seasons with the Cleveland Cavaliers, LeBron had twice been named Most Valuable Player. But to be considered one of the greatest players ever, LeBron knew he would have to add championships to his report card. The title finally came in 2012 as LeBron was named NBA MVP and Finals MVP. He dominated the playoffs averaging 30.3 points, 9.7 rebounds, and 5.6 assists.

Dwyane, who was selected fifth in 2003, had already led Miami to the 2006 NBA Championship. He averaged 34.7 points in the NBA Finals and was named Finals MVP. Still, Miami had slipped and Dwyane wanted that championship feeling back.

Dwyane, LeBron, and Chris were teammates on the 2008 United States Olympic gold-medal team and the 2006 FIBA World Championship team. They decided to see what they could do together in the NBA.

With the victory over Oklahoma in 2012, Miami's Big Three is showing just how much they're capable of.

LeBron James

HEAT 101

Did you know that in just three seasons the Heat went from having the fewest wins to playing for the NBA title in 2011?

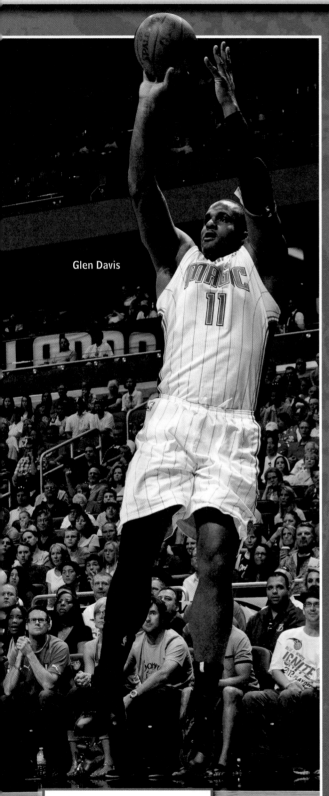

Glen Davis

First impressions aren't always what they seem. Glen Davis was already 5-6 and 160 pounds when he was nine years old. Because he was so tall, he was required to play against older children in senior basketball instead of the peewee league.

Frustrated, he would sometimes cry during practice. His coach would say, "Stop crying, you big baby." Glen doesn't cry anymore. At 6-9 and 289 pounds, "Big Baby" is one of the toughest power forwards in the NBA. And although fans still call him by his nickname, it is only because they know nothing could be further from the truth.

Being powerful is a good thing for Glen, because in the 2012–13 season the Orlando Magic will be relying on him more than ever. He is going to be asked to replace "Superman." With the Magic trading All-Star center Dwight Howard to the Los Angeles Lakers, Glen will be looking to expand his role with the team. It'a a job that he's ready for.

Glen stepped up his game in the 2011–12 Playoffs, averaging 19.0 points, 9.2 rebounds, and 1.2 assists. He also averaged 9.3 points and 5.4 rebounds in the regular season. "Big Baby" will now be the primary inside target for veteran point guard and teammate Jameer Nelson.

If Glen, who won a NBA Championship as a rookie with the Boston Celtics in 2008, can keep up that kind of production, the Magic will certainly have nothing to cry about.

MAGIC 101

Did you know that Glen attended Louisiana State University—the same college that former Orlando Magic center Shaquille O'Neal went to?

WASHINGTON WIZARDS

WIZARDS

John Wall

John Wall knew it was his turn. The two previous point guards who played for coach John Calipari—Derrick Rose and Tyreke Evans—had left after one college season to become NBA stars. So after just one All-American season at the University of Kentucky, John entered the 2010 NBA Draft and was picked first overall by the Washington Wizards.

In his NBA debut, John showed why he is considered the cornerstone of the Wizards' rebuilding program. John had 14 points, nine assists, and three steals. By his third game, he had become the second player to record at least nine assists in his first three NBA games. He also tied the franchise record with nine steals. Just over a month into his NBA career, John recorded his first triple-double by getting 19 points, 13 assists, and 10 rebounds against the Houston Rockets. He also had six steals.

In two NBA seasons, John has averaged 16.3 points and 8.2 assists, but the Wizards have struggled to win. A mid-season trade with Denver brought big man Nene Hilario to go to down low and in the 2012 Draft, the Wizards selected University of Florida sharpshooter Bradley Beal to team up with John. Add in veteran center Emeka Okafor and the continued development of 2011 first-round pick Jan Vesely, and John has the pieces around him to emerge as a star lead guard.

WIZARDS

Did you know that the franchise was called the Chicago Packers, the Chicago Zephyrs, the Baltimore Bullets, the Capital Bullets, and the Washington Bullets before becoming the Wizards in 1997?

NBA FINALS CHAMPIONSHIP WINNER
Miami Heat